Introduction

No one is too young for nursery rhymes. Babies respond to the *sounds* of words long before they can understand what the words mean. And if the words are rhythmic and musical, as all nursery rhymes are, so much the better. As they hear familiar rhymes over and over again, babies begin to anticipate and recognize the sounds—important first steps in the development of speech.

As children grow, nursery rhymes remain important. Finger rhymes and clapping rhymes like *Incey Wincey Spider* and *Pat-a-Cake* are a delightful way of helping toddlers develop motor skills and coordination. And what better way to introduce children to numbers and counting than with rhymes like *One, two, three, four, five, once I caught a fish alive?*

Rhymes can quiet and comfort as well as stimulate. Generations of children have been sent off to sleep with the gentle, soothing sounds of *Twinkle, Twinkle, Little Star* or *Rock-a-bye, Baby*. What would bedtime be without traditional rhymes and lullabies?

The intriguing stories, vivid language, and colorful characters of nursery rhymes fascinate young children and help expand their imagination. People who live in shoes and pumpkins, a cow that jumps over the moon, an egg that sits on a wall (and then falls off!), a ship with a crew of mice (and a captain that quacks!)… what a wonderful introduction to the infinite variety and joys of literature! And, for older children, what a rich source of ideas for storytelling, dressing up, and play-acting.

Most important, nursery rhymes are an intrinsic part of childhood. Children (and their parents) have loved these rhymes and kept them alive for centuries. Just as they were passed down to you by your parents, no doubt your children will pass them on to the next generation. They are every child's birthright, and part of the joy of childhood. Read them together, sing, play, laugh, and enjoy!

Ronne Randall

Ladybird Books Inc., Auburn, Maine 04210, U.S.A.
Published by Ladybird Books Ltd., Loughborough, Leicestershire, U.K.

© LADYBIRD BOOKS LTD 1994
LADYBIRD and the associated pictorial device are trademarks of Ladybird Books Ltd.
Printed in the United Kingdom

Ladybird

NURSERY RHYMES

Chosen by Ronne Randall
Illustrated by Peter Stevenson

Contents

Goosey, Goosey, Gander

Goosey, goosey, gander,
    Whither shall I wander?
Upstairs, downstairs,
    In my lady's chamber.
There I met an old man
    Who would not say his prayers.
I took him by the left leg
    And threw him down the stairs.

Jack and Jill

Jack and Jill went up the hill
To fetch a pail of water.
Jack fell down and broke his crown,
And Jill came tumbling after.

Up Jack got, and home did trot,
As fast as he could caper,
To old Dame Dob, who patched his nob
With vinegar and brown paper.

8

Mary Had a Little Lamb

Mary had a little lamb,
Its fleece was white as snow,
And everywhere that Mary went
The lamb was sure to go.

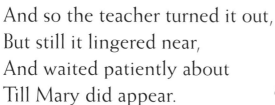

It followed her to school one day,
Which was against the rule.
It made the children laugh and play
To see a lamb at school.

And so the teacher turned it out,
But still it lingered near,
And waited patiently about
Till Mary did appear.

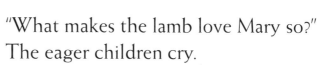

"What makes the lamb love Mary so?"
The eager children cry.
"Why, Mary loves the lamb, you know,"
The teacher did reply.

Baa, Baa, Black Sheep

Baa, baa, black sheep, have you any wool?
Yes, sir, yes, sir, three bags full.
One for the master, and one for the dame,
And one for the little boy who lives down the lane.

Little Boy Blue

Little Boy Blue, come blow your horn!
The sheep's in the meadow, the cow's in the corn.
Where is the boy who looks after the sheep?
He's under the haystack, fast asleep.
Will you wake him? No, not I!
For if I do, he's sure to cry.

Little Bo-peep

Little Bo-peep has lost her sheep,
And doesn't know where to find them.
Leave them alone, and they'll come home,
Bringing their tails behind them.

Little Bo-peep fell fast asleep,
And dreamt she heard them bleating.
But when she awoke, she found it a joke,
For they were still a-fleeting.

Then up she took her little crook,
Determined for to find them.
She found them indeed, but it made her heart bleed,
For they'd left their tails behind them.

Little Bird

Once I saw a little bird
Come hop, hop, hop.
So I cried, "Little bird,
Will you stop, stop, stop?"

I was going to the window
To say, "How do you do?"
But he shook his little tail,
And far away he flew.

Summer Breeze

Summer breeze, so softly blowing,
In my garden pinks are growing.
If you go and send the showers,
You may come and smell my flowers.

Mary, Mary

Mary, Mary, quite contrary,
How does your garden grow?
With silver bells and cockle shells,
And pretty maids all in a row!

Gray Goose and Gander

Gray goose and gander,
    Waft your wings together,
And carry the good King's daughter
    Over the one-strand river.

I Had a Little Nut Tree

I had a little nut tree,
    Nothing would it bear
But a silver nutmeg
    And a golden pear.

The King of Spain's daughter
    Came to visit me,
And all for the sake
    Of my little nut tree.

13

Bobby Shaftoe

Bobby Shaftoe's gone to sea,
Silver buckles on his knee.
He'll come back and marry me,
Bonny Bobby Shaftoe!

Bobby Shaftoe's fat and fair,
Combing down his yellow hair.
He's my love forevermore,
Bonny Bobby Shaftoe!

Rub-a-Dub-Dub

Rub-a-dub-dub,
Three men in a tub,
And how do you think they got there?
The butcher, the baker,
The candlestick-maker,
They all jumped out of a rotten potato,
'Twas enough to make a man stare.

I Saw a Ship A-Sailing

I saw a ship a-sailing,
     A-sailing on the sea,
And oh, but it was laden
     With pretty things for thee.

There were comfits in the cabin,
     And apples in the hold.
The sails were made of silk,
     And the masts were made of gold.

The four and twenty sailors
     That stood between the decks
Were four and twenty white mice
     With chains about their necks.

The captain was a duck
     With a packet on his back,
And when the ship began to move,
     The captain said, "Quack! Quack!"

Old King Cole

Old King Cole was a merry old soul,
And a merry old soul was he.
He called for his pipe, and he called for his bowl,
And he called for his fiddlers three.

Each fiddler he had a fiddle,
And the fiddles went tweedle-dee.
Oh, there's none so rare as can compare
With King Cole and his fiddlers three.

Sing a Song of Sixpence

Sing a song of sixpence,
A pocket full of rye.
Four and twenty blackbirds
Baked in a pie.

When the pie was opened,
The birds began to sing.
Wasn't that a dainty dish
To set before the King?

The King was in the counting house,
Counting out his money.
The Queen was in the parlor,
Eating bread and honey.

The maid was in the garden,
Hanging out the clothes,
When down came a blackbird
And pecked off her nose!

Little Miss Muffet

Little Miss Muffet
Sat on a tuffet,
Eating her curds and whey.
Along came a spider,
Who sat down beside her,
And frightened Miss Muffet away.

Curly Locks

Curly Locks, Curly Locks, wilt thou be mine?
Thou shalt not wash dishes, nor yet feed the swine,
But sit on a cushion and sew a fine seam,
And feast upon strawberries, sugar, and cream.

Little Tommy Tucker

Little Tommy Tucker
Sings for his supper.
What shall he eat?
White bread and butter.

How will he cut it
Without e'er a knife?
How will he marry
Without e'er a wife?

Little Jack Horner

Little Jack Horner sat in a corner,
Eating his Christmas pie.
He put in his thumb,
And pulled out a plum,
And said, "What a good boy am I!"

Little Betty Blue

Little Betty Blue
Lost her holiday shoe.
What can little Betty do?
Give her another,
To match the other,
And then she may walk in two.

The Queen of Hearts

The Queen of Hearts,
She made some tarts,
All on a summer's day.
The Knave of Hearts,
He stole the tarts,
And took them clean away.

The King of Hearts
Called for the tarts,
And beat the Knave full sore.
The Knave of Hearts
Brought back the tarts,
And vowed he'd steal no more.

The Lion and the Unicorn

The Lion and the Unicorn
Were fighting for the crown.
The Lion beat the Unicorn
All around the town.
Some gave them white bread,
Some gave them brown,
Some gave them plum cake,
And drummed them out of town.

Humpty Dumpty

Humpty Dumpty sat on a wall,
Humpty Dumpty had a great fall.
    All the King's horses
    And all the King's men
Couldn't put Humpty together again.

Ride a Cockhorse

Ride a cockhorse to Banbury Cross,
To see a fine lady upon a white horse.
Rings on her fingers and bells on her toes,
And she shall have music wherever she goes.

Hickory, Dickory, Dock

Hickory, dickory, dock,
The mouse ran up the clock.
The clock struck one,
The mouse ran down.
Hickory, dickory, dock!

Pussy Cat, Pussy Cat

Pussy cat, pussy cat, where have you been?
"I've been to London to visit the Queen."
Pussy cat, pussy cat, what did you there?
"I frightened a little mouse under the chair."

Six Little Mice

Six little mice sat down to spin,
Pussy passed by, and she peeped in.
What are you doing, my little men?
"We're weaving shirts for gentlemen."
Can I come in and cut off your threads?
"No, no, Mistress Pussy, you'd cut off our heads!"

I Love Little Pussy

I love little pussy, her coat is so warm,
And if I don't hurt her, she'll do me no harm.
So I'll not pull her tail, nor drive her away,
But pussy and I very gently will play.

Jack Sprat

Jack Sprat could eat no fat,
His wife could eat no lean,
And so between them both,
They licked the platter clean.

Jack ate all the lean,
Joan ate all the fat.
The bone they picked clean,
Then gave it to the cat.

Old Mother Hubbard

Old Mother Hubbard
Went to the cupboard
To fetch her poor dog a bone.
But when she got there
The cupboard was bare,
And so the poor dog had none.

There Was an Old Woman

There was an old woman tossed up in a blanket,
    Seventeen times as high as the moon.
But where she was going no mortal could tell,
    For under her arm she carried a broom.
"Old woman, old woman, old woman," said I,
    "Whither, oh whither, oh whither so high?"
"To sweep the cobwebs from the sky,
    And I'll be with you by and by!"

Hey, Diddle, Diddle

Hey, diddle, diddle,
The cat and the fiddle,
The cow jumped over the moon.
The little dog laughed
To see such sport,
And the dish ran away with the spoon!

The Man in the Moon
Came Tumbling Down

The man in the moon came tumbling down,
And asked the way to Norwich.
He went by south, and burnt his mouth
With supping cold pease porridge.

Pease Porridge Hot

Pease porridge hot,
Pease porridge cold,
Pease porridge in the pot,
Nine days old.

Some like it hot,
Some like it cold,
Some like it in the pot,
Nine days old.

One Misty, Moisty Morning

One misty, moisty morning,
When cloudy was the weather,
I met with an old man
Clothed all in leather,
Clothed all in leather,
With cap under his chin.
"How do you?" and "How do you do?"
And "How do you do?" again.

Doctor Foster

Doctor Foster went to Gloucester
    In a shower of rain.
He stepped in a puddle, right up to his middle,
    And never went there again.

The Old Woman Who Lived in a Shoe

There was an old woman who lived in a shoe,
She had so many children she didn't know what to do.
She gave them some broth without any bread,
Then scolded them soundly and sent them to bed.

Peter, Peter, Pumpkin Eater

Peter, Peter, pumpkin eater,
Had a wife and couldn't keep her.
He put her in a pumpkin shell,
And there he kept her very well.

Peter, Peter, pumpkin eater,
Had another, and didn't love her.
Peter learned to read and spell,
And then he loved her very well.

Georgie Porgie

Georgie Porgie, pudding and pie,
Kissed the girls and made them cry.
When the boys came out to play,
Georgie Porgie ran away.

Tweedledum and Tweedledee

Tweedledum and Tweedledee
    Agreed to fight a battle,
For Tweedledum said Tweedledee
    Had spoiled his nice new rattle.
Just then flew by a monstrous crow
    As big as a tar barrel,
Which frightened both the heroes so,
    They quite forgot their quarrel.

How Many Days?

How many days has my baby to play?
Saturday, Sunday, Monday,
Tuesday, Wednesday, Thursday, Friday,
Saturday, Sunday, Monday.
Hop away, skip away,
My baby wants to play,
My baby wants to play every day!

Dance to Your Daddy

Dance to your daddy,
My little babby,
Dance to your daddy,
My little lamb!

You shall have a fishy
In a little dishy,
You shall have a fishy
When the boat comes in!

Catch Him, Crow

Catch him, crow! Carry him, kite!
Take him away till the apples are ripe.
When they are ripe and ready to fall,
Here comes baby, apples and all!

Up, Up, Up

Here we go up, up, up.
And here we go down, down, down.
Here we go backwards and forwards,
And here we go round and round!

Dance, Little Baby

Dance, little baby, dance up high!
Never mind, baby, Mother is by.
Crow and caper, caper and crow,
There, little baby, there you go.
Up to the ceiling, down to the ground,
Backwards and forwards, round and round!
Dance little baby, and Mother shall sing,
With the merry chorus, ding-a-ding, ding.

Clap, Clap Handies

Clap, clap handies,
Mummy's wee one.
Clap, clap handies,
Till Daddy comes home,
Home to his bonny wee baby.
Clap, clap handies,
My bonny wee one.

Pat-a-Cake

Pat-a-cake, pat-a-cake, baker's man!
Bake me a cake as fast as you can.
Roll it and pat it and mark it with "B,"
And put it in the oven for baby and me.

Five Little Mice

This little mousie peeped within,
This little mousie walked right in!
This little mousie came to play,
This little mousie ran away!
This little mousie cried, "Dear me!
Dinner is done and it's time for tea!"

Two Little Dickey Birds

Two little dickey birds sat upon a hill,
One named Jack, the other named Jill.
Fly away, Jack! Fly away, Jill!
Come again, Jack! Come again, Jill!

Dance, Thumbkin, Dance

Dance, Thumbkin, dance,
Dance, ye merry men, every one.
But Thumbkin, he can dance alone,
Thumbkin, he can dance alone.

Dance, Foreman, dance,
Dance, ye merry men, every one.
But Foreman, he can dance alone,
Foreman, he can dance alone.

Dance, Longman, dance,
Dance, ye merry men, every one,
But Longman, he can dance alone,
Longman, he can dance alone.

Dance, Ringman, dance,
Dance, ye merry men, every one,
But Ringman, he can dance alone,
Ringman, he can dance alone.

Dance, Littleman, dance,
Dance, ye merry men, every one.
But Littleman, he can dance alone,
Littleman, he can dance alone.

Incey Wincey Spider

Incey Wincey Spider climbed up the water spout.
Down came the rain and washed the spider out.
Out came the sun and dried up all the rain,
And Incey Wincey Spider climbed up the spout again.

Here Sits the Lord Mayor

Here sits the Lord Mayor,
Here sit two men.
Here sits the rooster, and here sits the hen.
Here sit the little chicks,
And here they run in,
Chin-chopper,
Chin-chopper,
Chin-chopper, chin!

Round and Round the Garden

Round and round the garden,
Like a teddy bear.
One step, two steps,
Tickle you under there!

Teddy Bear, Teddy Bear

Teddy bear, teddy bear,
Turn around.
Teddy bear, teddy bear,
Touch the ground.

Teddy bear, teddy bear,
Climb the stairs.
Teddy bear, teddy bear,
Say your prayers.

Teddy bear, teddy bear,
Turn out the light.
Teddy bear, teddy bear,
Say good night.

Jack Be Nimble

Jack be nimble,
Jack be quick.
Jack jump over
The candlestick.

Jumping Joan

Here am I,
Little jumping Joan.
When nobody's with me,
I'm all alone.

Leg Over Leg

Leg over leg,
As the dog went to Dover.
When he came to a stile,
Hop! He went over.

Hogs in the Garden

Hogs in the garden, catch 'em, Towser.
Cows in the cornfield, run, boys, run.
Cats in the cream pot, run, girls, run.
Fire on the mountains, run, boys, run!

See-Saw, Margery Daw

See-saw, Margery Daw,
Jacky shall have a new master.
Jacky shall have but a penny a day,
Because he can't work any faster.

See-Saw, Sacra Down

See-saw, sacra down,
Which is the way to Boston town?
One foot up, the other foot down,
That is the way to Boston town.

This Is the Way the Ladies Ride

This is the way the ladies ride,
Nimble, nimble, nimble, nimble.
This is the way the gentlemen ride,
A gallop, a trot, a gallop, a trot.
This is the way the farmers ride,
Jiggety-jog, jiggety-jog.
And when they come to a hedge—they jump over!
And when they come to a slippery space—
They scramble, scramble, scramble,
Tumble-down Dick!

The Coachman

Up at Piccadilly, oh!
The coachman takes his stand,
And when he meets a pretty girl,
He takes her by the hand.
Whip away forever, oh!
Drive away so clever, oh!
All the way to Bristol, oh!
He drives her four-in-hand.

Ride, Baby, Ride

Ride, baby, ride,
Pretty baby shall ride,
And have a little puppy dog tied to his side,
And a little pussy cat tied to the other,
And away he shall ride to see his grandmother,
To see his grandmother,
To see his grandmother.

You Ride Behind

You ride behind and I'll ride before,
And trot, trot away to Baltimore.
You shall take bread, and I will take honey,
And both of us carry a purse full of money.

To Market

To market, to market, to buy a fat pig,
Home again, home again, jiggety-jig.
To market, to market, to buy a fat hog,
Home again, home again, jiggety-jog.

This Little Pig

This little pig went to market,
This little pig stayed home.
This little pig had roast beef,
This little pig had none.
And this little pig cried, "Wee-wee-wee,"
All the way home.

The Blacksmith

"Robert Barnes, my fellow fine,
Can you shoe this horse of mine?"
"Yes, indeed, that I can,
As well as any other man.
There's a nail, and there's a prod,
And now, you see, your horse is shod!"

Cobbler, Cobbler

Cobbler, cobbler, mend my shoe,
Get it done by half-past two.
Do it neat, and do it strong,
And I will pay you when it's done.

41

I'm a Little Teapot

I'm a little teapot,
Short and stout,
Here is my handle,
Here is my spout.
When I see the teacups,
Hear me shout,
"Tip me over and pour me out!"

Polly Put the Kettle On

Polly put the kettle on,
Polly put the kettle on,
Polly put the kettle on,
    We'll all have tea.

Sukey take it off again,
Sukey take it off again,
Sukey take it off again,
    They've all gone away.

Blow the fire and make the toast,
Put the muffins down to roast,
Blow the fire and make the toast,
    We'll all have tea.

Wash the Dishes

Wash the dishes, wipe the dishes,
Ring the bell for tea.
Three good wishes, three good kisses,
I will give to thee.

Handy Pandy

Handy Pandy, Jack-a-dandy,
Loves plum cake and sugar candy.
He bought some at the grocer's shop,
And out he came, hop, hop, hop!

Girls and Boys, Come Out to Play

Girls and boys, come out to play,
The moon is shining bright as day.
Leave your supper and leave your sleep,
And come with your playfellows into the street.
Come with a whoop, and come with a call,
Come with a good will, or come not at all.
Come, let us dance on the open green,
And she who holds longest shall be our queen.

Round About the Rosebush

Round about the rosebush,
    Three steps,
    Four steps,
All the little boys and girls
    Are sitting
    On the doorsteps.

Ring-a-Ring o' Roses

Ring-a-ring o' roses,
A pocket full of posies.
A-tishoo! A-tishoo!
We all fall down!

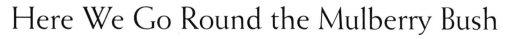

Here We Go Round the Mulberry Bush

Here we go round the mulberry bush,
    The mulberry bush, the mulberry bush.
Here we go round the mulberry bush,
    On a cold and frosty morning.

This is the way we wash our clothes,
    Wash our clothes, wash our clothes.
This is the way we wash our clothes,
    On a cold and frosty morning.

Pop Goes the Weasel!

Up and down the City Road,
    In and out the Eagle,
That's the way the money goes,
    Pop goes the weasel!

Half a pound of tuppenny rice,
    Half a pound of treacle,
Mix it up and make it nice,
    Pop goes the weasel!

Bangalorey Man

Follow my Bangalorey Man,
Follow my Bangalorey Man,
I'll do all that ever I can
To follow my Bangalorey Man.

We'll borrow a horse and steal a gig,
And round the world we'll do a jig,
And I'll do all that ever I can
To follow my Bangalorey Man.

The Muffin Man

Oh, do you know the muffin man,
    The muffin man, the muffin man?
Oh, do you know the muffin man
    That lives in Drury Lane?

Oh, yes, I know the muffin man,
    The muffin man, the muffin man.
Oh, yes, I know the muffin man
    That lives in Drury Lane.

47

Oranges and Lemons

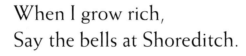

Oranges and lemons,
Say the bells of St. Clement's.

You owe me five farthings,
Say the bells of St. Martin's.

When will you pay me?
Say the bells of Old Bailey.

When I grow rich,
Say the bells at Shoreditch.

Pray, when will that be?
Say the bells of Stepney.

I'm sure I don't know,
Says the great bell at Bow.

Here comes a candle to light you to bed,
And here comes a chopper to chop off your head.

London Bridge

London Bridge is falling down,
　　Falling down, falling down.
London Bridge is falling down,
　　My fair lady.

Build it up with iron bars,
　　Iron bars, iron bars.
Build it up with iron bars,
　　My fair lady.

Iron bars will bend and break,
　　Bend and break, bend and break.
Iron bars will bend and break,
　　My fair lady.

Build it up with gold and silver,
　　Gold and silver, gold and silver.
Build it up with gold and silver,
　　My fair lady.

Gold and silver I've not got,
　　I've not got, I've not got.
Gold and silver I've not got,
　　My fair lady.

Then off to prison you must go,
　　You must go, you must go.
Then off to prison you must go,
　　My fair lady.

The Grand Old Duke of York

Oh, the grand old Duke of York,
He had ten thousand men.
He marched them up to the top of the hill,
And he marched them down again.
And when they were up, they were up.
And when they were down, they were down,
And when they were only halfway up,
They were neither up nor down!

The Big Ship Sails

The big ship sails on the alley, alley O,
The alley, alley O, the alley, alley O.
The big ship sails on the alley, alley O,
On the last day of September.

The captain said, "It will never, never do,
Never, never do, never, never do."
The captain said, "It will never, never do,"
On the last day of September.

The big ship sank to the bottom of the sea,
The bottom of the sea, the bottom of the sea.
The big ship sank to the bottom of the sea,
On the last day of September.

We all dip our heads in the deep blue sea,
The deep blue sea, the deep blue sea.
We all dip our heads in the deep blue sea,
On the last day of September.

One, Two, Buckle My Shoe

One, two, buckle my shoe,

Three, four, knock at the door.

Five, six, pick up sticks,

Seven, eight, lay them straight.

Nine, ten, a big fat hen,

Eleven, twelve, dig and delve.

Thirteen, fourteen, maids a-courting,

Fifteen, sixteen, maids in the kitchen.

Seventeen, eighteen, maids in waiting,

Nineteen, twenty, my plate's empty.

One for the Money

One for the money,
Two for the show,
Three to make ready,
And four to go!

I Love Sixpence

I love sixpence, jolly, jolly sixpence,
    I love sixpence as my life.
I spent a penny of it, I spent a penny of it,
    I took a penny home to my wife.

I love fourpence, jolly, jolly fourpence,
    I love fourpence as my life.
I spent twopence of it, I spent twopence of it,
    I took twopence home to my wife.

I love nothing, jolly, jolly nothing,
    I love nothing as my life.
I spent nothing of it, I spent nothing of it,
    I took nothing home to my wife.

My Father, He Left Me

My father, he left me, just as he was able,
One bowl, one bottle, one table,
Two bowls, two bottles, two tables,
Three bowls, three bottles, three tables,
Four bowls, four bottles, four tables,
Five bowls, five bottles, five tables,
Six bowls, six bottles, six tables.

Hot Cross Buns

Hot cross buns!
Hot cross buns!
One a penny, two a penny,
Hot cross buns!
If your daughters do not like them,
Give them to your sons.
One a penny, two a penny,
Hot cross buns!

Hickety, Pickety

Hickety, pickety, my black hen,
She lays eggs for gentlemen.
Sometimes nine, and sometimes ten,
Hickety, pickety, my black hen.

Chook, Chook, Chook

Chook, chook, chook, chook, chook,
　　Good morning, Mrs. Hen.
How many chickens have you got?
　　Madam, I've got ten.
Four of them are yellow,
　　And four of them are brown,
And two of them are speckled red,
　　The nicest in the town.

Magpies

I saw eight magpies in a tree,
Two for you and six for me.
One for sorrow, two for mirth,
Three for a wedding, four for a birth.
Five for England, six for France,
Seven for a fiddler, eight for a dance.

Jenny Wren

Jenny Wren last week was wed,
And built her nest in Grandpa's shed.
Look in next week and you shall see
Two little eggs, and maybe three.

The Dove Says, Coo, Coo

The dove says, "Coo, coo, what shall I do?
I can scarce maintain two."
"Pooh, pooh," says the wren, "I have got ten,
And keep them all like gentlemen."

Three Blind Mice

Three blind mice,
Three blind mice,
See how they run!
See how they run!
They all ran after the farmer's wife,
Who cut off their tails with a carving knife.
Did you ever see such a sight in your life,
As three blind mice?

White Feet

One white foot, buy him,
Two white feet, try him.
Three white feet, wait and see.
Four white feet, let him be.

Barber, Barber

Barber, barber, shave a pig,
How many hairs to make a wig?
Four and twenty, that's enough.
Give the barber a pinch of snuff.

Gregory Griggs

Gregory Griggs, Gregory Griggs,
Had twenty-seven different wigs.
He wore them up, he wore them down,
To please the people of the town.
He wore them east, he wore them west,
But he never could tell which he loved best.

Three Young Rats

Three young rats with black felt hats,
Three young ducks with new straw flats,
Three young dogs with curling tails,
Three young cats with demi veils,
Went out to walk with two young pigs
In satin vests and sorrel wigs.
But suddenly it chanced to rain,
And so they all went home again.

As I Was Going to St. Ives

As I was going to St. Ives,
I met a man with seven wives.
Each wife had seven sacks,
Each sack had seven cats,
Each cat had seven kits.
Kits, cats, sacks, wives,
How many were going to St. Ives?

(Answer: Only one — "I.")

Five Little Pussy Cats

Five little pussy cats sitting in a row,
Blue ribbons round each neck, fastened in a bow.
Hey, pussies! Ho, pussies! Are your faces clean?
Don't you know you're sitting there so as to be seen?

One, Two, Three, Four, Five

One, two, three, four, five,
Once I caught a fish alive.
Why did you let it go?
Because it bit my finger so.

Six, seven, eight, nine, ten,
Shall we go to fish again?
Not today, some other time,
For I have broke my fishing line.

Three Wise Men

Three wise men of Gotham
Went to sea in a bowl.
If the bowl had been stronger,
My song would be longer!

I Saw Three Ships

I saw three ships come sailing by,
     Come sailing by, come sailing by.
I saw three ships come sailing by,
     On New Year's Day in the morning!

And what do you think was in them then,
     Was in them then, was in them then?
And what do you think was in them then,
     On New Year's Day in the morning?

Three pretty girls were in them then,
     Were in them then, were in them then.
Three pretty girls were in them then,
     On New Year's Day in the morning.

One could whistle and one could sing,
     And one could play the violin.
Such joy there was at my wedding,
     On New Year's Day in the morning!

One Old Oxford Ox

One old Oxford ox opening oysters,

Two toads, totally tired, trying to trot to Tisbury.

Three thick thumping tigers taking toast for tea,

Four finicky fishermen fishing for finny fish.

Five frippery Frenchmen foolishly fishing for frogs,

Six sportsmen shooting snipe.

Seven Severn salmon swallowing shrimps,

Eight eminent Englishmen eagerly examining Europe.

Nine nimble noblemen nibbling nectarines,

Ten tinkering tinkers tinkering ten tin tinderboxes.

Eleven elephants, elegantly equipped,

Twelve typographical topographers typically translating types.

Mary at the Kitchen Door

One, two, three, four,
Mary at the kitchen door.
Five, six, seven, eight,
Eating cherries off a plate.

One's None

One's none,
Two's some,
Three's many,
Four's a penny,
Five's a little hundred.

Three Little Ghostesses

Three little ghostesses,
Sitting on postesses,
Eating buttered toastesses,
Greasing up their fistesses,
Up to their wristesses.
Oh, what beastesses,
To make such feastesses!

One, Two, Three

One, two, three,
I love coffee,
And Billy loves tea.
How good you be,
One, two, three,
I love coffee,
And Billy loves tea.

There Were Three Cooks

There were three cooks of Colebrook,
And they fell out with our cook.
And all was for the pudding he took
From the three cooks of Colebrook.

Four-Leaf Clover

One leaf for fame, one leaf for wealth,
One for a faithful lover,
And one leaf to bring glorious health,
Are all in a four-leaf clover.

One, He Loves

One, he loves; two, he loves;
Three, he loves, they say.
Four, he loves with all his heart;
Five, he casts away.
Six, he loves; seven, she loves;
Eight, they both love.
Nine, he comes; ten, he tarries;
Eleven, he courts; twelve, he marries.

There Were Two Wrens

There were two wrens upon a tree,
Whistle and I'll come to thee.
Another came, and there were three,
Whistle and I'll come to thee.
Another came, and there were four.
You needn't whistle any more,
For, being frightened, off they flew,
And there are none to show to you.

Two Crows

There were two crows sat on a stone,
One flew away and there was one.
The other, seeing his neighbor gone,
He flew away and then there were none.

Two Cats of Kilkenny

There once were two cats of Kilkenny,
Each thought there was one cat too many.
So they fought and they fit,
And they scratched and they bit,
Till, excepting their nails,
And the tips of their tails,
Instead of two cats, there weren't any.

Twelve Huntsmen

Twelve huntsmen with horns and hounds,
Hunting over other men's grounds.

Eleven ships sailing o'er the main,
Some bound for France and some for Spain,
I wish them all safe home again.

Ten comets in the sky,
Some low and some high.

Nine peacocks in the air,
I wonder how they all came there?
I do not know, and I do not care.

Eight joiners in Joiners' Hall,
Working with their tools and all.

Seven lobsters in a dish,
As fresh as any heart could wish.

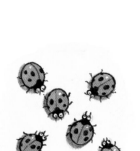

Six beetles against the wall,
Close by an old woman's apple stall.

Five puppies of our dog Ball,
Who daily for their breakfast call.

Four horses stuck in a bog,
Three monkeys tied to a clog.

Two pudding-ends would choke a dog,

With a gaping, wide-mouthed, waddling frog.

Twinkle, Twinkle

Twinkle, twinkle, little star,
How I wonder what you are!
Up above the world so high,
Like a diamond in the sky.

When the blazing sun is gone,
When he nothing shines upon,
Then you show your little light,
Twinkle, twinkle, all the night.

In the dark blue sky you keep,
And often through my curtains peep,
For you never shut your eye,
Till the sun is in the sky.

Jane Taylor

Star Light

Star light, star bright,
First star I see tonight,
I wish I may, I wish I might,
Have the wish I wish tonight.

I See the Moon

I see the moon,
And the moon sees me.
God bless the moon,
And God bless me.

The Man in the Moon

The Man in the Moon looked out of the moon,
    And this is what he said:
"Now that I'm getting up, 'tis time
    All children went to bed!"

Wee Willie Winkie

Wee Willie Winkie runs through the town,
Upstairs and downstairs in his nightgown,
Rapping at the window, crying through the lock,
"Are the children all in bed, for now it's eight o'clock!"

The Sandman

The Sandman comes,
The Sandman comes.
He has such pretty snow-white sand,
And well he's known throughout the land.
The Sandman comes.

All the Pretty Little Horses

Hush-a-bye, don't you cry,
Go to sleep, little baby.
When you wake, you shall have
All the pretty little horses.
Blacks and bays, dapples and grays,
Coach and six little horses.

Bossy-Cow, Bossy-Cow

Bossy-cow, bossy-cow, where do you lie?
In the green meadows, under the sky.

Billy-horse, billy-horse, where do you lie?
Out in the stable, with nobody nigh.

Birdies bright, birdies sweet, where do you lie?
Up in the treetops, ever so high.

Baby dear, baby love, where do you lie?
In my warm cradle, with Mama close by.

Come, Let's to Bed

"Come, let's to bed,"
Says Sleepy-head.
"Tarry awhile," says Slow.
"Put on the pan,"
Says Greedy Nan,
"Let's sup before we go."

A Glass of Milk

A glass of milk and a slice of bread,
And then good night, we must go to bed.

Sippity Sup

Sippity sup, sippity sup,
Bread and milk from a china cup.
Bread and milk from a bright silver spoon,
Made of a piece of the bright silver moon!
Sippity sup, sippity sup,
Sippity, sippity sup!

Go to Bed First

Go to bed first, a golden purse;
Go to bed second, a golden pheasant;
Go to bed third, a golden bird.

Go to Bed Late

Go to bed late,
Stay very small.
Go to bed early,
Grow very tall.

Come to the Window

Come to the window,
My baby, with me,
And look at the stars
That shine on the sea!
There are two little stars
That play at bo-peep
With two little fishes
Far down in the deep,
And two little frogs
Cry, "Neap, neap, neap,
I see a dear baby
That should be asleep!"

Sweet and Low

Sweet and low, sweet and low,
　　Wind of the western sea.
Low, low, breathe and blow,
　　Wind of the western sea!
Over the rolling waters go,
Come from the dying moon, and blow,
　　Blow him again to me;
While my little one, while my pretty one, sleeps.

Sleep and rest, sleep and rest,
　　Father will come to thee soon;
Rest, rest, on mother's breast,
　　Father will come to thee soon.
Father will come to his babe in the nest,
Silver sails all out of the west,
　　Under the silver moon;
Sleep, my little one, sleep, my pretty one, sleep.

Alfred, Lord Tennyson

79

Up the Wooden Hill

Up the wooden hill
    To Bedfordshire,
Down Sheet Lane
    To Blanket Fair.

Diddle, Diddle, Dumpling

Diddle, diddle, dumpling, my son John
Went to bed with his trousers on.
One shoe off, and one shoe on,
Diddle, diddle, dumpling, my son John.

Babyland

How many miles to Babyland?
Anyone can tell.
Up one flight, to your right,
Please to ring the bell.

What do they do in Babyland?
Dream and wake and play,
Laugh and crow, fonder grow,
Jolly times have they.

Rock-a-bye

Rock-a-bye baby, thy cradle is green,
Father's a nobleman, Mother's a queen.
Betty's a lady and wears a gold ring,
And Johnny's a drummer, and drums for the King.

Hush, Little Baby

Hush, little baby, don't say a word,

Papa's going to buy you a mockingbird.

If that mockingbird won't sing,

Papa's going to buy you a diamond ring.

If that diamond ring turns brass,

Papa's going to buy you a looking glass.

If that looking glass gets broke,

Papa's going to buy you a billy goat.

If that billy goat won't pull,

Papa's going to buy you a cart and bull.

If that cart and bull turn over,

Papa's going to buy you a dog named Rover.

If that dog named Rover won't bark,

Papa's going to buy you a horse and cart.

If that horse and cart fall down,

You'll still be the sweetest little baby in town.

French Cradle Song

If my boy sleep quietly,
He shall see the busy bee,
When it has made its honey fine,
Dancing in the bright sunshine.

If my boy will slumber,
Angels without number
Will draw near, so fair and bright,
For they only come at night.

Sleep, Oh Sleep

Sleep, oh sleep,
While breezes so softly are blowing.
Sleep, oh sleep,
While streamlets so gently are flowing.
Sleep, oh sleep!

Sleep, oh sleep,
While birds in the forest are singing.
Sleep, oh sleep,
While echoes with music are ringing.
Sleep, oh sleep!

Sleep, oh sleep,
While angels are watching beside thee.
Sleep, oh sleep,
May blessings forever betide thee.
Sleep, oh sleep.

Hush-a-bye, Baby

Hush-a-bye, baby, lie still in the cradle,
Mother has gone to buy a soup ladle.
When she comes back, she'll bring us some meat,
And Father and baby shall have some to eat.

Dear Baby, Lie Still

Hush-a-bye, baby, lie still with thy daddy,
Thy mammy has gone to the mill,
To get some meal, to make a cake,
So pray, my dear baby, lie still.

Rock-a-bye, Baby, Rock

Rock-a-bye, baby, rock, rock, rock,
Baby shall have a new pink frock!
A new pink frock and a ribbon to tie,
If baby is good and does not cry.

Rock-a-bye, baby, rock, rock, rock,
Listen, who comes with a knock, knock, knock?
Oh, it is pussy! Come in, come in!
Mother and baby are always at home.

Raisins and Almonds

To my baby's cradle in the night
Comes a little goat all snowy-white.
The goat will trot to the market,
While Mother her watch does keep,
Bringing back raisins and almonds.
Sleep, my little one, sleep.

Rock-a-bye, Baby, on the Treetop

Rock-a-bye, baby, on the treetop,
When the wind blows, the cradle will rock.
When the bough breaks, the cradle will fall,
And down will come baby, cradle and all.

Sleep, Baby, Sleep

Sleep, baby, sleep,
Thy father guards the sheep,
Thy mother shakes the dreamland tree,
And from it fall sweet dreams for thee.
Sleep, baby, sleep.

Sleep, baby, sleep,
Our cottage vale is deep.
The little lamb is on the green,
With woolly fleece so soft and clean.
Sleep, baby, sleep.

Sleep, baby, sleep,
Down where the woodbines creep.
Be always like the lamb so mild,
A kind and sweet and gentle child.
Sleep, baby, sleep.

Cradle Song

Lullaby and good night, with roses bedight,
With lilies bedecked is baby's wee bed.
Lay thee down now and rest,
May thy slumber be blessed.
Lay thee down now and rest,
May thy slumber be blessed.

Lullaby and good night, thy mother's delight,
Bright angels around my darling shall stand.
They will guard thee from harms,
Thou shalt wake in my arms.
They will guard thee from harms,
Thou shalt wake in my arms.

Johannes Brahms

The Evening Is Coming

The evening is coming, the sun sinks to rest,
The birds are all flying straight home to the nest.
"Caw," says the crow as he flies overhead,
"It's time little children were going to bed!"

The butterfly, drowsy, has folded its wing.
The bees are returning, no more the birds sing.
Their labor is over, their nestlings are fed.
It's time little children were going to bed.

Here comes the pony, his work is all done,
Down through the meadow he takes a good run.
Up go his heels and down goes his head.
It's time little children were going to bed.

Now the Day Is Over

Now the day is over,
Night is drawing nigh.
Shadows of the evening
Steal across the sky.

Down with the Lambs

Down with the lambs,
    Up with the lark,
Run to bed, children,
    Before it gets dark.

91

Quiet the Night

Quiet the night,
Soft is the breeze.
Dim is the light
Of the faraway moon.

Sleep, children, sleep,
Be not alarmed,
Angels on guard
Will keep you unharmed.

Golden Slumbers

Golden slumbers kiss your eyes,
Smiles awake you when you rise.
Sleep, pretty baby, do not cry,
And I will sing you a lullaby.
Rock them, rock them, lullaby.

Good Night

Good night,
Sleep tight,
Wake up bright
In the morning light
To do what's right
With all your might.